How to Get Your Kid to Move Out

Disclaimer

This is an adult discussion, about a subject, in which even the best of parents frequently foul up. How do we get our young adult children to live somewhere else and be financially independent? This is just a discussion. It is not to be used as a substitute for competent Personal or Family Therapy. No counseling service is implied, by you reading this small book.

This is just one parent commiserating and reflecting with another. You do not get to blame me for the consequences of your own parenting decisions. If things go wrong at this delicate developmental stage in your child's life; seek competent professional support.

The Nightmare Scenario #1

All identifying characteristics have been changed in this very true story.

Frank lives in a mother-in-law apartment, which his elderly parents had constructed 10 years before in the garage. Inside the house proper, is a toilet and shower, just to the left when you walk in. Frank is a well-mannered young man who has been down on his luck. Most recently, his car died, and was impounded. Because he didn't have a car to get to work he lost his job and the Wilder Beast Burger restaurant. He was doing better until his car problem, because he was a shift manager. Now he just sits in his room and plays video games. It is a good thing he has mom and dad to fall back on.

He pays no rent and never showers at the house. Often he just pees in a bottle instead of going in the house. His sanitation issue aside, this is not a new problem for Frank. It is a lifestyle because he is 28 years old. His parents loath him and don't know what to do.

My Answer

It is time for Frank to go. He can crawl into a hole somewhere else or make a life for himself. Set a date and then change the locks. If he wants to get all legal with his parents, he wasn't paying rent anyway. Keep it friendly but you must save his life and give him some dignity.

Supply him with community resources and crisis numbers but send him on his way. If they can't do it they should hire somebody else to speak for them; but do it. Park the car in the garage.

They might feel guilty but the time for wallowing in guilt is long gone. Besides, guilt won't change anything. We all make mistakes. Move on.

He will survive and even prosper if he so chooses. It is completely up to him. Welcome to the real world Frank. It is actually a beautiful place to be.

Post Script

Frank never did move. Both of his parents died of poor health exacerbated by stress within three years of this story.

Nightmare Scenario #2

All identifying details have been changed in this true story

Holly is young woman who has the unfortunate luck being fertile. She is pregnant with her second child and has been too sick to work. Money is extremely tight as her mother is the sole supporter of the household. Holly's dad left for parts unknown ten years ago. With a 1 year old grandson living with her and a granddaughter on the way Holly's mom is at the end of her rope. Holly is twenty years old. What should mom/grandma do?

My Answer

There are two issues. They should be considered separately.

First Holly must go to counseling. Even though she uses birth control pills and condoms; these things are not 100% effective and Holly now has Herpes, a life-long sexually transmitted disease. Clearly Holly must abstain from sex until such time as she is married and can afford a baby. Perhaps spiritual counseling can support in leading a chaste life.

The family has a Catholic background maybe she should see a priest and a young mom support group. She needs to be hooked up with every support available for young single moms including WIC the federal food program for moms and children.

As for the dead beat dads, they need to be sued for child support. Most states will assist with doing this and collecting the money.

The next issue gets tougher. What should grandma do about everybody living with her? Does grandma really have the stamina to help raise the kids for the next 18 years? No.

So after the next baby arrives, social services are in place, and Holly is working, everybody must move out. Grandma can help out by doing the occasional emergency baby sit, and Holly should move on with her life. If she learns that sex makes babies, she will do fine

If the burden of child rearing is too great she should consider adoption or even open adoption.

Post Script

Holly did keep the kids and did move. Recently she completed law school and was hired by a small but growing firm in a major city. The kids are happy and healthy and are now 9 and 10 years old. Holly continues to look for love in all the wrong places.

Personal Reflection

When our kids emancipate we want them to do better than us. Sometimes this happens but often they do only as well or even worse than us. The way they were raised conditions them to what they call normal.

For example, when I was growing up, in my earliest memories, we always had cable TV in our house. So as an adult I tried to always have cable wherever I lived, including the couple decades I lived on a boat. It just did not feel like home without the TV running and a hundred channels to watch.

Only when I turned 52 years old did I experiment with quiet and saving the $2000 a year cable bill. It took a real effort to break out of what felt normal and good. The same things happen in other aspects of our lives.

Another example is career choice. Often it is replicated in our young. Being in a family of lawyers or teachers or welfare recipients just feels normal. Our offspring often unconsciously copy us.

The Outcome In Mind

The final goal of every parent should be independent offspring. Although most parents are very conscious of this goal almost all of us are hesitant about some aspect of emancipation.

After all we have spent almost two decades of our lives trying to meet our child's basic needs. Now we are having a fight in our mind and our heart about sending them off into the world. But there is really is no healthy option. It is not good for you and it isn't good for them if they stay at home forever.

I am fifty two years old and the single most common question asked by my peers is, "How did you get your kids to move out?" I just tell them that the conversation started when they were in middle school. The move out date was set five years ahead of time.

If you let them sit on your sofa playing video games instead of working and producing; eventually they will be lazy. They need to get busy living and start preparing for their emancipation.

When is a good time to start talking with your child about them moving out?

I think it is important to at least mention your plans for their emancipation before high school. Ideally they can make plans with you. They need to see that this a time of preparation. That is why they need to: do well in school, learn to drive, and get a job now.

School

School is the last time they will get an education for free. They should be finding ways to maximize this free gift from our society. School is the place where they can gain work skills which will serve them well in the years to come.

Every child should take typing. Keyboarding is essential in the age of technology and computers. They should learn to touch type at 80 words per minute.

Every child should learn to drive. Every child should take an auto shop class. We drive all the time but how many how many of us are really good at defensive driving. How many of us can do simple repairs and maintenance on our cars. Drivers Education should continue at home where we can give them the benefit of our mistakes and experiences.

Every child should take Health Class as a conversation starter at home for discussions on sexuality and morality. If we leave sex education up to the school our children may actually think that the nightmare of "anything goes" is ok.

If they are sexual active before marriage and practicing safer sex still a percentage of our young people will get sexually transmitted diseases like AIDS and or make a baby. Planned Parenthood will be happy to take care of the abortion in my state for children as young as thirteen without parental consent. Sex is too important of a topic to leave with school.

You may feel really uncomfortable talking to your child but you must buck up and do it. If you tell them you are nervous it may take some of the discomfort out it for both of you. The topic of sex is literally life or death. If you don't know about sex, study up! Besides, the whole topic is really about rather simple biology. More importantly, it is about complex relationships. The topic of relationships should go on all through the teen years.

College and Vocational Training

If your child has the aptitude let them start planning for college and how they are going to pay for it. Perhaps they should start in one of the programs like Running Start in high school. Running Start lets a student take up to two years at the local community college. The student goes for free and graduates high school with a two year college degree. Community colleges have had to dumb down their courses so much that this is really possible for the mature high school student to succeed.

Maybe vocational training is just what your child needs. He or she can gain and document the entry level skills necessary for dozens of good paying jobs. My outboard repairman charges $90 an hour plus parts, and my auto mechanic labor fees are astronomical. A savvy high school student can go right into the work force after high school. It is absolutely sad when a kid graduates and has no skills except video game playing.

Video Gaming is the Enemy

I am completely against having video games in the home because they waste valuable time that could be used for emancipation activity like studying. Parents say it is just a little harmless fun but it almost never stays that way. Children should have other hobbies and friends and play outside.

Almost nobody agrees with me but I think that video gaming steals motivation from the young. It is a kind of the marijuana of the present generation. In any case after a child graduates from high school no video games should be allowed in the house. It might make it a little easier for them to move out.

In many places there are state sponsored internships in the trades. I kid with a car, a drug free test, and crime free background can start working a in a trade at half pay. This can be as much as $22.50. After 2 or 4 years depending on the trade they become a union certified Journeyman and get the full union wage!

Money for College

Kids who want to go to college need to get serious about how they are going to pay for it. There are five kinds a funding. They are: gifts, grants, scholarships, work study, and Student Loans. These resources can all be accessed through the high school counselor, the admissions counselor at the college and a website called FastWeb.com.

The student should register and at the website and spend at least 2 hours a week responding to funding opportunities. I recently wanted some last minute funding for school. I applied on a Sunday and had the $3,000 I needed on Saturday.

Just say no to Student Loans! Twenty three years ago I took out a $15,000 loan. I am still paying on it. I have paid $37,000 and I still have $9,000 dollars to go. It is not a good deal and defaulting in some states is a felony! If a student takes out a loan don't co-sign for it. If the student defaults they will go after you and even bankruptcy will not excuse your student loan.

Where will my child live?

Sometimes if there is room, an adult child might decide to live in the basement and pay rent. This is an ok temporary arrangement if a young adult is doing some post high school training or schooling.

It must be time limited and for a purpose. Maybe the young adult is saving up money for a special training program in windmills in another state. As long as he/she pays for their share of the utilities, food, and $100 rent; I don't have a concern.

They must get used to the idea that they must live within their means. If they lose their fast food job; they have to go get another one. If they lose their good better paying job; they have to go get a fast food job. If their car breaks down they must fix it or ride the bus.

Adversity can unleash the creative power of the human being. One young adult I know couldn't keep a job until she worked in a cannery in Alaska. Another young adult seemed to drift aimlessly until he joined a Christian Mission group going to the South Seas. Still another young person I know got a paid internship with the state and now is well employed as an IT professional.

If a parent rescues their adult offspring from financial hardship; they offspring have no dignity or motivation to ever be independent.

When I graduated from college and had no job; I soon moved onto a boat and paid less than $75 a month for shelter. I enjoyed it so much that I live aboard for two decades. See "How and Why I Lived Aboard" by James Nugent at Amazon.com.

For work I was employed in YMCA and CYO recreation programs, until I completed a Master's degree in Counseling and Community Psychology. Two weeks after graduate school I became a school counselor. If my mom had made me weak by trying to take care of my needs after college; I doubt if I would be as happy and productive as I am today.

The Empty Nest Syndrome

Almost all parents go through this to some degree. After our kids moved out my wife said it was like a knife in her heart. I kept yelling a greeting to the kids every time I came through the front door for a year. Their emancipation was relatively painless and eventually we stopped calling them all the time.

We fondly look forward to their birthdays and holidays and someday we have hope for grandchildren. Every few months we get together with them and their girlfriends and have a board game party or a dinner. It is fun.

Over the last 5 years we have found even greater pleasure in relating to our soon to be 24 year old twin sons. I don't know if this is possible but I think I really like them even more now that they are grown up:>

We didn't know if they would be gone forever or just a few months when they left. If they came back I made it clear that they would live under the same house rules and they were only welcome until they were ready to try freedom again. That would be a very short time. A job was lost and a car was wrecked but they never came back. They are having too much fun!

This is not so true for millions of families across the country. The offspring never left the nest. The adult children have no real desire or motivation to take concrete steps to move.

I was shocked when I worked as counselor in private practice, that whole families were still living as a single family unit with adult children still using parents as a sole source of support.

I naively suggested that a mom should ask her free loading 26 year old son to move out when she exploded with defensiveness and exclaimed "he needs me." I said that I owed it to her to talk about the issue because it was one of the reasons she was depressed and suicidal.

She said we could talk about anything but her son. Eventually counseling with me failed because we could not talk about one of her major issues.

However things got better for her when her son got 20 years in prison for indecent liberties with a 12 year old neighbor girl. The whole hideous affair shows us how important it is that we treat our adult children like adults.

A Summary of "How to Get Your Kid to Move Out."

Understand that emancipation is a natural and normal step.

Make moving out a happy topic.

Talk about moving many years ahead of time.

Live the Teen Years in the context of preparation for moving out.

Insist that certain skills be attained for moving out.

Insist that a certain amount of money be saved for moving out.

Put your mixed feelings aside. You are saving their life.

Get them to take an active part in the planning of moving out.

Don't make a big deal about it when the day comes.

It is a natural and normal thing to move out.

Keep your doubts to yourself. You don't want to sabotage him/her.

If they come back, they can stay only a short while and then must go again.

Taking Care of You

Eventually the day will come when your last offspring is out of the house and then it is time to begin to take care of yourself. Maybe you would like to down size your home and put the profits in the bank for retirement. Maybe the big two story home costs too much to heat. Maybe the yard is too big. Maybe you would like to move to the San Juan Islands or Lake Havasu?

For the first time in decades you have a chance to really mix things up. If you are in good health and you have time to save; invest for your retirements.

Don't wait until you retire to start living. I read somewhere that the average male only lives 18 months after retirement. If the federal government raises the social security retirement age just 3 years, it will solve a lot of their budget problems. Most of us will be dead. Your home is your major resource for retirement. Spend it wisely! Get competent financial advice. However I have always been a little suspicious of any advisor who invests your money for a fee and gets paid even if they lose your money!

I also have grave concerns about the Social Security System going bankrupt. They send me a notice estimating the date this will happen every year. I bet you can't say what the date is! Plan accordingly. You don't want to live with your kids in your old age!

Parenting is tricky stuff. Don't give up if an adult child is living on your sofa. Cancel the cable and ban video games from the house. Then help them make a plan. If that doesn't work make a plan for them and set a date and don't forget to change the locks:>

All we can do is prudently do our best and God will have to take care of the rest.

James Nugent 2013

Other Books by James Nugent

How I Sailed From Olympia to The San Juan Islands, and Returned Safely

An Alternative Boating Guide to Southern Puget Sound

How and Why I lived Aboard

Kayaking Budd Inlet in South Puget Sound

I Speak Esperanto

The Rainbow Road and Other Signs of God's Love

Living an Abundant Life, Within Your Means

Social Jujitsu and Powerful Principles for Managing Social Conflict

Blackjack on My Small Budget

A Little Benedictine Oblate Manuel

Without Speech

All things work

Loving Time with Your Creator

Personal Adventures in a Life of Learning

The Good News about Being Catholic

E-book Writing and Overcoming Barriers to Creativity

E-book Writing and Organizing Your Ideas

My Forty Days For Life 2013

How to Sail in the Winter

Lifestyle Reality Observing

Twenty Hours under The Sea

Notes and Reflections

Printed in Great Britain
by Amazon

25932921R00015